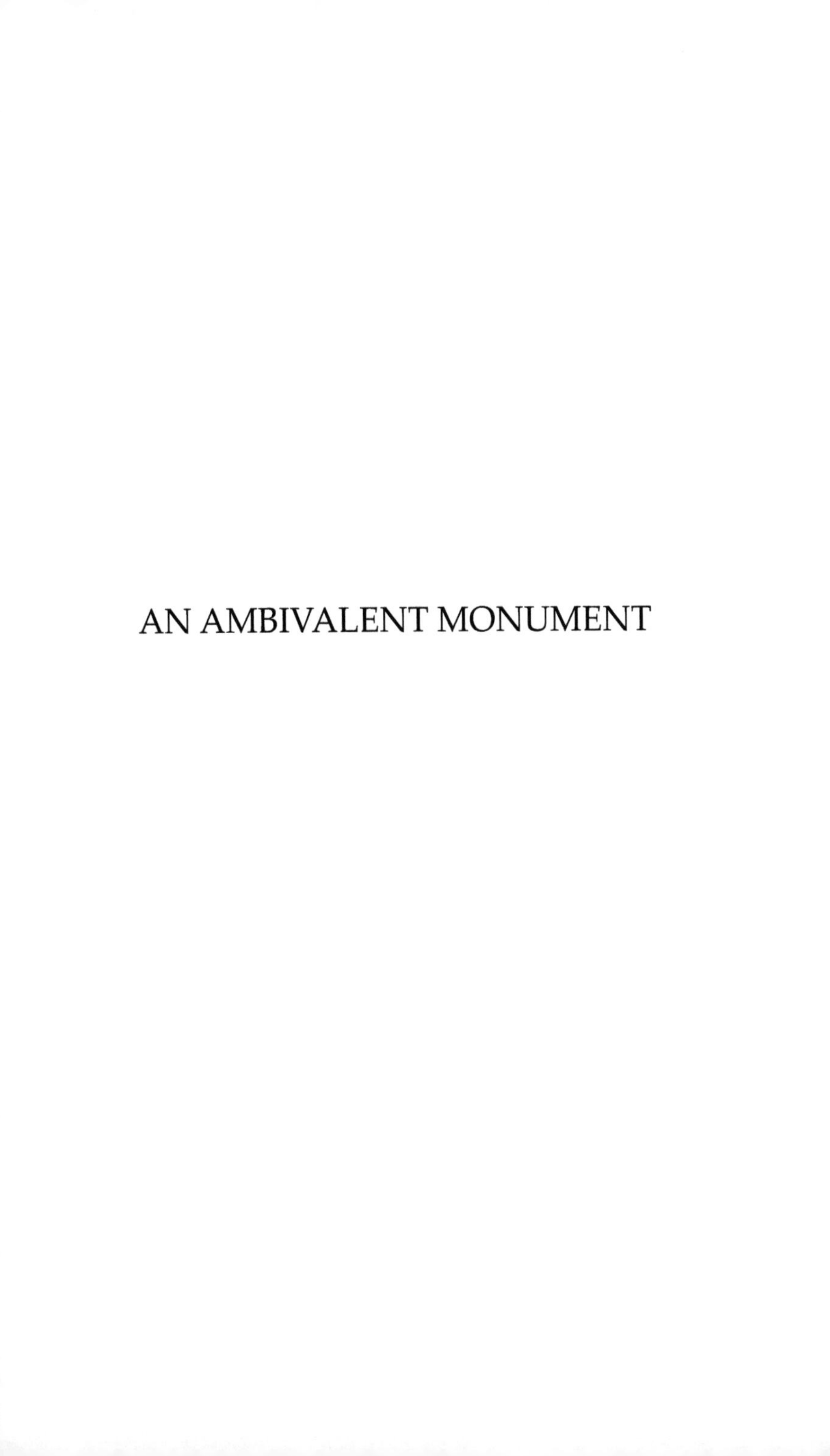

AN AMBIVALENT MONUMENT

AN AMBIVALENT MONUMENT

THOMAS MORISON

EDITIONS ZORZAL

MONTRÉAL, QUÉBEC

An Ambivalent Monument
Copyright © 1998, 2012 by Thomas Morison

Library and Archives Canada Cataloguing in Publication

Morison, Thomas, author
An ambivalent monument : tragicomedy : a play / by Thomas Morison.

Originally published in HTML format (Montréal : Kasey Productions, 2013).

ISBN 978-0-9920750-6-4 (pbk.)

I. Title.

PS8576.O6838A86 2014 C812′.54 C2014-905822-5

Editions Zorzal
Printed in Canada

An Ambivalent Monument was first presented by Le Nouveau Théâtre Anglais at Théâtre La Chapelle, Montréal, on the 12th of February 2003 with the following cast:

KEIR	Diana Fajrajsl
LOUISE	Laura Mitchell
HOWARD	Harry Standjofski
THERESA	Emma Stevens
VERN	Stéphane Zarov

Production Stage Manager Kathryn Cleveland
Designed by Vincent Lefèvre
Sound design by Stéphane Volet
Lighting design by Natalie Goyer
Directed by Michael Springate

We acknowledge the support of the Canada Council for the Arts.

Nous remercions le Conseil des arts et des lettres du Québec de son soutien.

Characters

THERESA 50
HOWARD 40
KEIR 40
LOUISE 35-40
VERN 35-40

ACT I

(A room. A window. A table. A pile of rocks upstage. Lights fade up, back-lighting. Howard is seated in the dark. His silhouette is visible. He stands. He is looking for something. He bumps into the table. Enter Keir. She turns on a light. She looks out the window.)

HOWARD: Those are stratus clouds and if they came crashing down from the sky. I wouldn't bother to tell you.

KEIR: Were you looking for that?

(She points to a rock that is on the table.)

HOWARD: What?

KEIR: No?

HOWARD: No.

KEIR and HOWARD: No.

KEIR: Why not put it where it belongs?

HOWARD: I might.

KEIR: You could throw it in the pile.

HOWARD: I don't know where it came from. Don't ask me. You weren't going to ask me I hope. Then maybe I've sinned for the pleasure of it, and sometimes sin's a pleasure and sometimes it's not a pleasure at all.

KEIR: What were you looking for?

HOWARD: A note that was on the table.

KEIR: A note?

(She picks up the rock. Finds a piece of paper under it. Gives it to him. He looks at it.)

HOWARD: This isn't it. I had written on it.

KEIR: Yes, I erased it for the paper. I intended to use it.

HOWARD: Did you notice what was written on it?

KEIR: No.

HOWARD: I don't remember what I wrote.

KEIR: If you wrote it you should remember it.

HOWARD: You don't remember what you might have read?

KEIR: It was illegible. Your writing's terrible.

HOWARD: So nothing. It was something I was supposed to do today.

KEIR: That shouldn't be difficult to remember.

HOWARD: I have no way of knowing that.

KEIR: Then when was the last time you thought of what you would be doing today?

HOWARD: Yesterday. Wouldn't you think?

KEIR: But you won't ask me to ask you what you were thinking.

HOWARD: No.

KEIR: Though maybe you were going to be thinking of planning for tomorrow.

HOWARD: I'd have done that today.

KEIR: So perhaps you could go out then.

HOWARD: Out? Where?

KEIR: Wherever you like.

HOWARD: No.

(Sound of a clay pot breaking offstage.)

KEIR: She's busy already it seems like.

HOWARD: Watering her plants, but it rains enough without having to water them constantly. It was raining all night. It was strange. I looked out the window and saw her last night, watering her plants in the rain. I called out, "Why are you watering your plants in the rain?"

KEIR: Oh?

HOWARD: It was raining hard. She didn't hear me. You didn't hear me either. You were sound asleep.

KEIR: I must have been exhausted.

HOWARD: You were snoring is why you didn't hear me.

KEIR: I was sleepy, obviously, I had to sleep.

HOWARD: There was nothing you could do about it. You couldn't help yourself, but that's no excuse.

KEIR: I disturbed you without wanting to.

HOWARD: As I listened to you in bed thundering away, I was thinking — since you want to know what I was thinking, I was thinking... I was trying to come up with my plans whatever they might have been and I thought I would like to do something terrible to a loved one, something abominably horrible, perverse and disgusting.

(He picks up from the table a twig. It has a few leaves.

It is a cutting from a bay laurel tree. He examines it, plucks a leaf from it, lets the leaf drop.)

KEIR: To me?

HOWARD: To you?

KEIR: To me?

HOWARD: No. Yes. Maybe. We might not subscribe to ambivalence and that would make one not to decide otherwise. But that is difficult to do when there is so much uncertainty, yet there's the science that almost explains what is what, but it's not what it might be. There is a reason not to be impressed as to how the laws of nature are being obeyed and the way that natural phenomenon adheres to the laws of nature is not reassuring, though if that's not the case then why not accept what is what and come to an agreement that there are things that can be recognized for what they are or for what is perhaps otherwise. But what? *(Holds the twig up, examining it.)* Maybe plants or animals, natural things, that aren't what they should be. But then why be impressed by observable facts, for example, why be impressed by the instincts of plants?! What is natural flowering flora. Quivering in the wind in time with the circadian rhythm. Pollinated by restless hummingbirds. *(Holds up the twig.)* Or of insects, could be another example: ants, for example. Then imagine we're taken up by observing an ant, who's working away like someone who has too much to do, like so many of us do. But who would be interested? Who's interested that that ant is another ant that is a part of the work of the other ants, when it's an ant crawling along the ground and with a bread crumb on her back and the fact that she gets the crumb back to her hill and down her hole is not an interesting spectacle. I'd just as soon step on the ant, on the mother ant, while she is giving birth to her young. So these ants are eating us alive. They are eating the flesh off our bones. People are killing us. People are killing people. Then I hope that we do not subscribe to ambivalence. I hope that we do not subscribe maybe otherwise. *(Sniffs at the leaves.)* It's a bay leaf. *(Sniffs it.)* It's a bay leaf. God, I am tired.

KEIR: You must be.

(A man enters, crosses the stage in front of them and exits.)

HOWARD: Then I wouldn't have mentioned that the other day, a gentleman came to speak about you and me. He was a history teacher, taught history. He was a historian.

KEIR: Taught history, really? That's interesting. What history was that?

HOWARD: *Ours.* He came in and told me that the end of history had come.

KEIR: They all always say the same thing.

HOWARD: That it's all over.

(Sound of pot fragments being shuffled.)

Then what is she doing?

KEIR: Potting.

(Keir looks out the window.)

HOWARD: And who would want to pick up the pieces?

(Sound of the pot fragments. Keir raises the blinds, light streams in, he reacts to it. She opens the window.)

HOWARD: Close the window.

KEIR *(calling out the window)*: Louise.

LOUISE *(offstage)*: Yes, hello. I broke a pot.

KEIR *(calling out the window)*: Oh well.

LOUISE: It was hot.

KEIR: What a rain last night.

LOUISE *(offstage)*: Now the sun is out.

KEIR *(calling out the window)*: It's getting hot?

LOUISE *(offstage)*: It's hot on the pots.

KEIR *(calling out the window)*: Hot pots then.

LOUISE *(offstage)*: They are.

KEIR *(to Howard)*: The pots are hot.

LOUISE *(offstage)*: That's why I dropped it.

KEIR *(calling out the window)*: So the sun is bright.

LOUISE *(offstage)*: Hopefully the wind will come up.

KEIR *(calling out the window)*: Is it supposed to?

LOUISE *(offstage)*: Hopefully.

HOWARD: She shouldn't come in, if that is what you have in mind. I am not dressed.

KEIR *(calling out the window)*: Louise, come in, come in if you'd like.

(He kicks off his shoes.)

HOWARD: Fine, I shall remove my clothes? Should I?

LOUISE *(offstage)*: Thank you.

(Keir closes the window and lowers the blinds. Howard removes his shirt.)

KEIR: Too hot for you?

(He drops his trousers to the floor. Throws his shirt at Keir. Louise enters.)

LOUISE: Hello.

HOWARD: Hello, excuse me, I was getting dressed.

LOUISE: Forgive me.

(Keir throws his shirt back at him.)

HOWARD: It's all right. It was time to get dressed. I wasn't going to stand around in my underwear all day, although I might as well. *(He puts on his clothes. They watch him dress.)* And you're busy?

LOUISE: I am keeping busy. *(Referring to the rock.)* You found it. I knew you'd be interested in it or was hoping you would be. I thought you would like it, that you could add it to your collection.

HOWARD: I don't collect any more.

LOUISE: You don't?

HOWARD: No, I don't.

LOUISE: When did you stop?

HOWARD: When people started throwing them at me.

KEIR: There were too many piling up.

HOWARD: Then are your plants doing well?

LOUISE: They are doing very well, though it has been raining more than is needed.

KEIR: It has, hasn't it?

HOWARD: You're not over-watering them?

LOUISE: No, I don't think so.

HOWARD: You do a lot of watering, that doesn't kill them?

LOUISE: Well, if they stay alive I'll water them. If they die I stop. It keeps me busy.

HOWARD: But why busy one's self unnecessarily?

LOUISE: For the pleasure of it I guess.

HOWARD: The pleasure of it?

LOUISE: Then just to keep busy maybe.

HOWARD: But are there not other pleasures more pleasurable and maybe necessary?

LOUISE: Well yes, but one can't have everything in this world.

HOWARD: You wouldn't want to?

LOUISE: What?

HOWARD: Have everything? No?

LOUISE: Well, no.

HOWARD: You wouldn't?

LOUISE: Can't see how. No.

HOWARD: Why not?

LOUISE: It's asking for a bit much.

HOWARD: Why settle for less is what I ask?

KEIR: He's not in a very pleasant mood today.

LOUISE: On a day like today.

HOWARD: It's too hot.

LOUISE: Well, I have been starting slow in the morning myself.

HOWARD: You must stay up late at nights.

LOUISE: I do. Yes.

KEIR: Would you like to sit down?

LOUISE: Thank you.

KEIR: Please. Take my chair.

LOUISE: I can't stay for long.

KEIR: Sit down.

LOUISE: I won't stay long. *(She sits.)* I can't stay long. Yes, I am busy.

(pause)

HOWARD: So your father. Is he still hanging on for dear life?

LOUISE: Well, yes, but he's going down quickly, last night he asked, "Is it time to die? May I die?" What could I say? "No, you can't die. It's not your time, father." But in any case, I'm prepared. I have taken care of the practicalities. Everything seems to be ready. I'll have enough flowers to put on his grave, which he doesn't approve of, and I don't know if I'll put them on or not. And with everything else that is all I seem to worry about, whether or not I should obey his last wishes. He hates flowers because they attract bees. I don't know what to do.

KEIR: You're doing what you can.

HOWARD: He wouldn't know the difference either way. If there were flowers or bees.

(pause)

LOUISE: Everything else is ready, I hope. I've bought a plot and written up the invitations and the thank-you notes for the condolences. I'm ready. But it's the waiting for it to happen that keeps me thinking that I must have forgotten something. *(pause)* At least he's resting comfortably. *(pause)* I've done everything I could to make him comfortable. *(pause)* I am doing everything I can to make his death easier for him.

KEIR: What else could you do?

LOUISE: Well, I'd best go see how he's doing.

KEIR: If you need anything.

(Louise walks to the door.)

LOUISE: Thank you.

KEIR: Bye.

(Louise exits. Pause.)

That was awkward.

HOWARD: I don't know if it was.

(Sound of voices is heard offstage approaching, rushing by, disappearing. The words are unintelligible.)

HOWARD: Do you realize she came in without us

knowing it. We didn't know she came in to put it there. *(Pointing at the rock.)* And I told you I didn't know anything about it. So I didn't hear her come in. As if I don't have enough reason to be suspicious of everything.

KEIR: There's nothing you can do about it now.

HOWARD: I wouldn't suggest there was. That is not what I'm suggesting.

KEIR: Then I might suggest that we open a window, and if you want you can look out it and get some fresh air at least.

(Voices pass by from the opposite direction.)

HOWARD: I asked you to close it.

KEIR: I'm going to open it for myself.

HOWARD: Don't open the window.

(She opens the window. Sticks her head out.)

KEIR: A little fresh air would be good for us, for you.

HOWARD: Close it.

KEIR: What is it now, Howard?

HOWARD: Close the window. I am not asking you nicely. Close it.

KEIR: When I have finished looking out if it I will.

HOWARD: Close it!

(She slams the window shut.)

And lock it.

KEIR: It doesn't lock.

HOWARD: That is probably how she got in. She opened the unlocked window and sneaked in.

KEIR: You know, with a little faith you could ask if you were loved by me, by God. Yet you'd rather have no faith.

HOWARD: Yes, I probably would rather not.

KEIR: None at all.

HOWARD: Of course not, what do you expect?

(Voices pass again. Knocking at the door. The noise of the knocking is maybe that of a small drum or a woodblock.)

KEIR: Someone's there knocking at the door.

HOWARD: You are going to answer it. I know you are. Then if I were to remove my clothes again that wouldn't stop you from answering it.

(He unbuttons his shirt, stops, buttons it up. Knocking becomes louder.)

KEIR: I don't recognize the knock. Yes, I'll see who it is.

(She answers the door. Mumbling offstage.)

Howard. The man here, I don't believe it. You wouldn't either. The man is a beggar.

HOWARD: What? Who is?

KEIR *(offstage)*: If you don't want to believe me, come and look.

(Keir enters.)

HOWARD: You want me to?

KEIR: I almost don't believe it myself. Come.

HOWARD: What does he want?

KEIR: Money.

HOWARD: No.

(Keir exits.)

KEIR *(offstage to the beggar)*: I'm sorry.

HOWARD: Why not offer a drink?

KEIR *(offstage)*: It's money he's after.

HOWARD: Though we don't have anything worth drinking, but a beggar can't be choosy.

KEIR *(offstage)*: He doesn't drink.

HOWARD: A beggar who doesn't drink.

(She closes the door. Re-enters. Knocking at the door. She exits.)

KEIR *(offstage)*: He's returned. *(To beggar.)* We have nothing. We would like to help. But we've nothing. You understand?

(She closes the door. Re-enters. Vern walks across the stage in front of them, pushing his bicycle. He is holding a bundle of helium balloons.)

The man wanted to make sure I didn't have anything to give to him. Apparently people don't give anything the first time so he has to ask two or three times. I told him there was nothing we could do.

HOWARD: You didn't think I heard you?

KEIR: He was a little deaf.

HOWARD: I'd have thought she was a woman.

(Loud knocking.)

KEIR: No, that's a man.

(Keir exits.)

HOWARD: For Christ's sake!

KEIR *(offstage)*: No.

HOWARD: He must be drunk.

KEIR *(offstage)*: NO. I TOLD YOU. NO. I SAID NO. WE HAVE NOTHING. NOTHING. I'LL NOT REPEAT MYSELF. I ALREADY TOLD YOU. GO AWAY.

(She re-enters.)

He didn't want to leave. Perhaps I ought to have given him something.

HOWARD: Then it's not too late. Go after him. He couldn't have gone too far.

KEIR: No, he was running. Maybe we should be more charitable, because if we're not known for being charitable, what are we known for?

(Vern walks his bicycle again across the stage in front of them. Exits.)

Vern.

HOWARD: Vern.

KEIR: Balloons.

HOWARD: He isn't stopping, don't stop Vern. Do not stop.

KEIR: Doesn't look like it. *(A bicycle bell rings offstage.)* He's warning the children.

HOWARD: He wouldn't want to mow them down or he's letting them know that he's going to run them over. *(Bicycle bell rings offstage.)* Then a few days ago, last week, a short woman went by on a bicycle, riding slowly, a tiny little woman, who might as well have been walking and was in no hurry, should have been walking, if you're going to ride that slowly why not walk? This tiny midget of a woman on a bike too big for her, which made her look even more ridiculous, and I was ready to say to her. "Ride the bike or get off and walk!"

KEIR *(humouring him)*: From the circus, was she a little person from the circus?

HOWARD: I shouldn't think so.

KEIR: There used to be midgets in the circus who rode bicycles.

HOWARD: Not in the modern circus.

KEIR: And because you're short doesn't mean you shouldn't ride a bike, and it was said to me I was too short and I never learned how to ride.

HOWARD: What are you saying?

KEIR: I was told I was too short.

HOWARD: You were misled.

KEIR: I always thought so.

HOWARD: You're not that short.

KEIR: No, I didn't think so either.

HOWARD: Even if you were, look at me, I am shorter

than the average giant and I rode around.

KEIR: For you, but when I was young I wasn't very tall.

HOWARD: You weren't a midget!

KEIR: No, I wasn't, and it shouldn't have made that much difference. I was just shorter than the average.

(Bicycle bell rings offstage. Beat.)

HOWARD: So you never rode a bike, humph, well, and I never knew that. So then, if we had gone to Holland. *(Bicycle bell rings offstage.)* You wouldn't have been able to ride on a bike with me, tandem along the dykes, the two of us in Holland. *(Bicycle horn honks offstage.)* How we would have been amongst the tulips, next to the windmills, riding a bike off into the sunset on the top of a dyke with the ocean crashing underneath us. We could have gone. But now we would only look silly riding around on bicycles, even in Holland. Though I hear it is a good country to die in. To be happy in Holland and then die whenever you want. It's the perfect country, a kid takes his finger out of a dyke and everyone dies.

(Vern rides by in front of them. Rings a bicycle bell.)

Then a drunk bear in a circus could ride better than that.

KEIR: He's coming.

HOWARD: Vern.

KEIR: He's going.

(Vern re-enters and rides by.)

He's coming.

(Vern re-enters and rides by.)

KEIR: He's going.

HOWARD: You're going to invite him in? You'll call out the window to him.

KEIR: I could if you'd like.

HOWARD: Why not leave the door open and the window, and we could take the roof off and knock down the walls, so that it's an open house for anyone who wants to stop by whenever it's convenient for whoever the hell it is.

(Louise rides by on a bicycle.)

Louise.

KEIR: It was. *(Looks out the window.)* The clouds are clearing. Then the children are tying their wishes onto balloons and are sending them up again.

HOWARD: It's too bad that it's not up to us to stop them, Keir.

(Sound of Vern standing up his bicycle outside. She goes to greet him.)

KEIR *(offstage)*: Come in.

VERN *(offstage)*: Hello, hello.

(Vern enters with the bundle of helium balloons. Pieces of paper are tied to the strings on the balloons. One balloon is bigger than the others.)

VERN: Hello.

HOWARD: Hello Vern.

VERN: Hello.

HOWARD: Vern.

VERN: It is me. I was out riding and thought I'd come and tell you what has been happening. These are interesting times.

KEIR: You are out riding.

VERN: I saw Louise.

KEIR: Yes, we just saw her.

VERN: You've seen the balloons. I got a few myself and I remembered when you had those balloons. When was that?

HOWARD: We don't remember.

(Vern separates the big balloon from the others. Gives the bundle of balloons to Keir.)

KEIR: Thank you.

(Vern lets go of the large balloon. They watch it. It rises.)

VERN: So what's happening, it's terrible and it looks like there will be fighting, as there is all kinds of discontent and I am afraid we are going to have to worry about the coming events. It's not going to be promising.

HOWARD: I've been saying that for years.

VERN: You were right.

HOWARD: Storm clouds are gathering on the horizon?

VERN: It's not safe anywhere. People are being attacked in their homes, in their beds, or as they go about their business as usual. Then what I believe is the trick, is to keep a distance to what is happening. Operate behind the scenes and count on one's luck if it's there and I have been lucky.

HOWARD: You are not well-informed.

VERN: Part of the problem is that no one knows what is going on.

HOWARD: That's not so unusual.

VERN: Then those who do have some information aren't telling anyone else. Meanwhile the rest of us are afraid something is going to happen and we don't know why.

HOWARD: You are on the right side?

VERN: Well, I hope I will be lucky.

HOWARD: That may not work for you.

VERN: If I am to be lucky now is the time.

HOWARD: If I were you I wouldn't put too much faith in justice. It might not be on your side.

VERN: I'm cautious, you know.

HOWARD: Don't want to be too cautious.

VERN: I know when I have to be aggressive.

HOWARD: Wouldn't want to be too aggressive either.

VERN: No.

HOWARD: This is all theoretical of course.

VERN: Well —

HOWARD: Theory is only so good up to a point.

VERN: Yes, the trick is knowing when to put it into

practice.

HOWARD: At times you can be too late.

VERN: Or too early.

HOWARD: It's always hard to tell.

VERN: That's why I have to be lucky.

HOWARD: I hope you are.

VERN: I would be dead by now if I weren't. But here I am living proof of my own good fortune.

HOWARD: For that you have my blessing.

VERN: Your blessing would be appreciated.

HOWARD: I hope everything turns out well for you.

VERN: For all of us.

HOWARD: I am sure it will.

VERN: Well, I wanted to warn you. That's why I came. Not that I want you to worry needlessly.

HOWARD: We thank you.

VERN: Thought you should be warned. Then I hope you like the balloons. It's the little things that matter when nothing else does. *(pause)* But in the meanwhile I am out enjoying the fine weather. Hot out.

KEIR: Are you thirsty?

VERN: I am, yes.

KEIR: Howard isn't enjoying himself. He finds the weather too hot.

VERN: You've never liked the hot weather.

HOWARD: No.

VERN: You should try riding a bicycle. It keeps you cool.

KEIR: He won't do anything. He has just been sitting there. He's typical of those who don't like hot weather.

VERN: But if you go out in the hot weather you get used to it.

KEIR: Here is some water.

(Keir gives Vern a glass of water.)

VERN: Yes, I should be going, and if you need anything. Let me know. I'll keep you informed.

KEIR: Bye Vern.

VERN: Bye, see you soon, any time.

(Vern exits.)

HOWARD: He took the glass with him.

(Keir takes a note from a balloon.)

KEIR: There's a wish. Could it come true? *(Reads note.)* "Dear sir and madam, if you sneeze, God bless you." *(Reads another note.)* "I wish people who were unhappy could see me smiling." There's an idea. That has to be a happy child. Some children are like that even when young. *(Reads another note.)* "I wish people who were sick were never contagious." *(Reads another note.)* "I wish I was a hero, a hero for you." So do I, don't you?

HOWARD: No. It says that?

KEIR: His writing isn't very good, but he's probably just learning to write.

HOWARD: I wouldn't agree with that premise at all.

KEIR: You wouldn't?

HOWARD: For the sake of having an argument I would simply disagree.

KEIR: Why?

HOWARD: For the sake of disagreeing, but then I don't mean a word of what I'm or was saying which meant nothing of what I might have meant. So then everything I've ever said up until now is meaningless noise, and I'm not just saying so to be contrary to my own way of thinking.

KEIR: Maybe you are.

HOWARD: I'm being brutally honest.

KEIR: Should I have to put up with you?

HOWARD: Don't put up with me.

KEIR: You're making me angry, Howard.

HOWARD: You've annoyed me.

KEIR: If you never sleep again you will deserve it.

HOWARD: Why don't you go out yourself?

KEIR: I will.

HOWARD: Why don't you?!

(pause)

KEIR: Yes, I am going to take a walk. I am going out.

(She exits, leaving the door open. A light comes up on the rock.)

HOWARD: Ah. *(He picks up a note with a wish, looks at*

it.) I wish you hadn't erased my note. Then what the hell am I going to do? What am I going to do? Nothing.

(Louise bicycles across the front of the stage. He watches her.)

ACT II

(Louise rides in through the door. Dismounts. Stands in the middle of the room holding the bike.)

LOUISE: I rode by earlier.

HOWARD: That was you.

LOUISE: The door was open so I thought I'd ride in, crazy of me. I didn't want to leave it outside. I was afraid it might be stolen.

HOWARD: Yes, it would have been.

LOUISE: Keir's out?

HOWARD: Gone for good.

LOUISE: I've heard you arguing.

HOWARD: We get angry at times.

LOUISE: But you know when they're gone it's too late.

HOWARD: Ah.

LOUISE: When they are gone for good you miss them. *(pause)* Then it's days like today when everyone comes out on their bicycles that I like to go out for a ride myself. I have always wanted to ride a bike around naked, in broad daylight, down a busy street, past a monastery full of young seminarians.

HOWARD: Why don't you?

LOUISE: I'm going to. I have promised myself I would, except I have to get my courage up first, and by the time I do I'll be old, which wouldn't be interesting for anyone. *(pause)* So the roads are rough, washed out in places.

HOWARD: From the rain.

LOUISE: And it's hilly in spots. I don't much like riding up the hills. Going down them is the way to go.

HOWARD: Easier?

LOUISE: It is.

HOWARD: Is that a Dutch bike?

LOUISE: What?

HOWARD: Japanese?

LOUISE: I ought to know.

HOWARD: The Dutch make excellent bikes as do the Japanese if you can get one that's big enough, on the other hand the Dutch bikes are too big.

LOUISE: The seat's French.

HOWARD: That's a tickler.

LOUISE: Yes, it is.

HOWARD: Comfortable?

LOUISE: It is comfortable.

HOWARD: It's a man's bicycle.

LOUISE: But I ride it like a woman. *(pause)* This was my husband's. *(pause)* He had dreamt of being a professional cyclist. *(pause)* My poor husband, when I think about him I have an urge to go and dig him up and lie in his bones and cry. *(pause)* So you see, you do miss them when they're gone, and soon I will miss my father.

HOWARD: You'd dig him up?

LOUISE: I've wanted to.

HOWARD: I'd like to see that.

LOUISE: I'd probably rather be alone at the time.

(pause)

HOWARD: Well, I could spy on you.

LOUISE: As long as I didn't notice.

HOWARD: I have noticed.

LOUISE: Oh?

HOWARD: You have poise.

LOUISE: I have poise?

HOWARD: Your poise is.

LOUISE: Your wife and I are friends.

HOWARD: She wouldn't mind.

LOUISE: But I am lonely at times.

HOWARD: So I can respond to suggestions that you'd care to make and can initiate others you may never have thought of.

LOUISE: Well, I never have trouble instructing a man as to what it is that I like.

HOWARD: What do you like?

LOUISE: I like.

HOWARD: What exactly?

LOUISE: I like, oh.

HOWARD: Yes?

(pause)

LOUISE: I like to be scratched. When I have an itch. The worse the itch the more I like to be scratched. Vigorously.

HOWARD: If you have an itch.

LOUISE: Even if I don't itch I still like to be scratched.

HOWARD: Do you itch?

LOUISE: We never have been very friendly to each other you and I.

HOWARD: We could make up for that.

LOUISE: Then up until now I have been faithful to the memory of my deceased husband.

HOWARD: Even the greatest of people are eventually forgotten.

LOUISE: I have always thought you were heartless, amusing, though mean and vicious.

HOWARD: They're just moods.

LOUISE: They are terrible moods.

HOWARD: Then... I saw you last night in the rain, dripping, wet, in the rain. The water was steaming off of you.

LOUISE: I saw you looking.

HOWARD: I was going to go out.

LOUISE: Why didn't you?

HOWARD: I thought you'd have run off.

LOUISE: I would have stayed.

HOWARD: I shouted out to you, but you didn't hear me.

LOUISE: I didn't? No.

HOWARD: Will you be out tonight?

LOUISE: I finish my watering very late.

HOWARD: It has been raining a lot.

LOUISE: Yes, it comes in from the continent.

(pause)

HOWARD: Then have you been to Holland?

LOUISE: Yes.

HOWARD: Have you?

LOUISE: Several times.

HOWARD: I've always wanted to go to Holland.

LOUISE: It rains a lot.

HOWARD: It does.

LOUISE: I went when I was a little girl with my father. He's Dutch. He was a bicycle repairman when young, and he fixed this bike for me.

HOWARD: A true Dutchman then?

LOUISE: He also repaired planes, in the Dutch Air Force.

HOWARD: A Flying Dutchman.

LOUISE: A test pilot.

HOWARD: What fine people are the Dutch. What a great country.

LOUISE: I appreciate the flowers they grow.

HOWARD: It's the only place in the world where I've wanted to go. But I am afraid if I go I will never come back.

(pause)

LOUISE: Our conversation is agreeable.

HOWARD: I agree.

(pause)

LOUISE: If nothing else from now on we can at least be more pleasant to each other.

HOWARD: Yes, I would hope to be more friendly.

LOUISE: My father is dying.

HOWARD: It sounds like he had a good life.

LOUISE: He fixed this bike for me. *(She gets on the bike.)* I better ride some more before it rains again.

(She rides circling the table.)

HOWARD: Why are you leaving so soon?

LOUISE: I think I should.

HOWARD: Stay.

LOUISE: No, I thought I'd leave.

HOWARD: Then I would join the seminary myself.

LOUISE: Would you?

HOWARD: If I had to.

LOUISE: You won't have to.

HOWARD: No?

(Louise exits.)

Christ! *(beat)* I don't trust her. I don't trust myself. I trust no one. I'm talking to myself.

(Noise outside. Door opens.)

Hello? *(pause)* Who is it? *(pause)* Hello. Is that you?

KEIR *(offstage)*: Yes.

HOWARD: Why didn't you answer?!

KEIR *(offstage)*: I knew it was you.

HOWARD: What if it had been someone else?

KEIR *(offstage)*: It's you Howard, I know it's you.

HOWARD: Why did you come back so soon?

(Enter Keir.)

KEIR: Come in. I've invited Theresa.

(Enter Theresa.)

THERESA: Hello.

HOWARD: What do you want?

THERESA: I didn't want to come.

HOWARD: Why did you?

THERESA: I won't stay long.

HOWARD: No, don't stay long.

THERESA: I have been invited but am unwelcome.

HOWARD: You would have known that before you came.

THERESA: I should go.

HOWARD: Goodbye.

THERESA: Except I thought I'd say a few things. One is that you have made Keir an unhappy woman.

HOWARD: And I am an unhappy man.

THERESA: She wanted me to have a word with you and I agreed. Though I knew there would be no point in me saying much.

HOWARD: You were right.

THERESA: She says you are being more difficult than usual.

HOWARD: Because I am not a happy man.

THERESA: You have no reason to be.

HOWARD: No.

THERESA: Still not sleeping?

HOWARD: No.

THERESA: There must be a reason why you haven't.

HOWARD: There is.

THERESA: Keir wanted me to give you some advice. And I'd have some advice if I thought you'd listen, but you don't listen, so I won't bother.

(Theresa moves to exit.)

KEIR: You are going to leave?

THERESA: I wish there was something I could say, but what? Nothing helpful. *(to Howard.)* Then now that there is trouble and unrest, you ought to be pleased.

Maybe your predictions will come true. You'll be right. That would make you happy.

HOWARD: That would be unfortunate.

THERESA: Right! But completely wrong.

KEIR: Don't go, let me get you something to drink?

THERESA: No, I'm leaving.

KEIR: I know he is inexcusable. I am sorry.

THERESA *(to Keir)*: What will do any good?

(Keir accompanies Theresa out the door.)

KEIR *(offstage)*: It's from the lack of sleep.

THERESA *(offstage)*: Is that it?

KEIR *(offstage)*: Bye. *(Keir re-enters. Pause.)* Howard.

HOWARD: I was beginning to think she was going to over-stay her welcome.

KEIR: Howard.

HOWARD: Is there anyone else coming?

KEIR: Vern. I saw him on the road, and he thought he might stop by on his way back from where he was going.

HOWARD: You asked him to. You invited him to come along to give me advice.

KEIR: He might.

HOWARD: You asked him to come along to give me advice.

KEIR: No.

HOWARD: You've asked Vern to advise me.

KEIR: He asked if there was anything he could do.

HOWARD: You thought he would come by, that he might as well.

KEIR: I don't know if he will.

HOWARD: So he is coming along? Vern are you out there? There he is.

(Sound of a bicycle approaching. Bicycle bell rings.)

VERN!

VERN *(offstage)*: Hello.

HOWARD: That you Vern?

VERN *(offstage)*: Hello, I am standing up my bike.

HOWARD: What are you doing?

(Vern enters.)

VERN: Well, I was just standing up my bike.

(Sound of a bike falling over offstage. Vern moves to exit.)

HOWARD: Leave it Vern, it will be all right.

VERN: I'll leave it then.

HOWARD: Did you see that lady that went out on the lane?

VERN: I did, yes.

HOWARD: Did she say anything to you?

VERN: Hello. She seemed friendly.

HOWARD: You don't know her.

VERN: I should have?

HOWARD: No.

VERN: I don't think I know her.

HOWARD: She is an old friend of the family and Keir invites her in. Why would we invite her to come in?

VERN: If she's a family friend –

HOWARD: There's a reason, and what would you say to me if I asked you for advice?

VERN: What would you like to hear?

HOWARD: No, what would you tell me?

VERN: I don't know, that would depend probably.

HOWARD: Of course it would.

VERN: It's hard to say in that case.

HOWARD: When would we have met, Vern?

VERN: When?

HOWARD: When?!

VERN: When do you mean?

HOWARD: How long ago was it?

VERN: A long time, I don't know.

HOWARD: In that time what have we really said to each other that meant anything?

VERN: Oh, there must have been something at one time.

HOWARD: But what do you know about a philosophy?

VERN: A philosophy, oh, I should know something about a philosophy.

HOWARD: No, you don't.

VERN: I think I do. Not that I believe that everyone can be enlightened all of the time.

HOWARD: You put up with my abuse.

VERN: I do, and if we can't abuse our friends.

KEIR *(to Vern)*: Don't encourage him.

HOWARD: He can encourage me.

KEIR: Leave him be.

HOWARD: I abuse my friends, because no one can stop me. Can you? Can you stop me?

VERN: Well, I don't take it too seriously.

KEIR: Add to your sins, Howard.

HOWARD: One or two more wouldn't matter.

VERN: What sins?

(beat)

HOWARD: I have sinned.

VERN: Oh, that's too bad.

HOWARD: No, it's all right, I've only just realized it is all. That I've always wanted to kill innocent people and just for fun.

VERN: Oh well, I'm sorry anyway.

HOWARD: Then I'm sure you have your share of them.

VERN: Not that I know of.

HOWARD: I should think you have sinned, Vern, probably more than you know.

VERN: No, no.

HOWARD: What of your business dealings? I'd wager there's sin in that line of work.

VERN: I don't make enough profit for that.

HOWARD: And by your associates, one can be guilty by association.

VERN: My associates are fine people.

HOWARD: Not by association. So you want to give me advice. Why is it in all these years we have never known what you do?

VERN: Because what I do is a mystery to myself. Part of the mystery. Life. That's my philosophy.

HOWARD: Philosophy! You know what futility is? What it amounts to?

VERN: Oh...

HOWARD: What is it?

VERN: Yes, I do.

HOWARD: I'll explain futility to you, what it is, it's an idea, a construction and I've been working on it so that we can see what it amounts to, and the idea is that futility is a monument which is something that is imaginary or real, more real than imaginary, as most things are when you imagine they're real. And this idea holds its own and can withstand criticism because it's a free standing structure and a wonder to marvel at architecturally, modest in form, yet conceptually large in spirit, as to how the forms of its shape have taken shape and been formed. And as can be imagined with such a project it's not to be expected that the usual procedural steps in construction are applicable, not at all, no plans have been drawn up or are being followed and as a result, as it all goes along there are stages of the process that go backwards and forward, and at times in both directions, which has turned out to be impractical, but then the monument is of no real practical use, no monument is, though it looks practical. Then there are fixtures as are found in the more useful kinds of buildings, except that nothing works. The doors don't open, the windows non-transparent. And so recently the last of what anyone has heard is that the work that is being done has accomplished nothing. Nevertheless, it does seem to be progressing somehow or other, though unfortunately the appreciation of the monument and the idea behind it has not been well received, in fact no one likes it. It is hated by everyone who is living, except me, and I wouldn't be surprised if it is torn down, and then we will have to build it up again, and then it will be torn down again, because no one realizes that it is futile to fight against futility. No reason that I could defend. But if nothing else, at least I can say that I have said this before. I have said many times that this is a pointless gesture. And now I would like to say so again. I'd like to say that if there is a revolution then we will all die for nothing. The same as all the other idiots who died in all the other futile revolutions. Who in their right mind would want to die for what they believe in? I'd rather change my mind or lose it. I'd rather lose my mind.

VERN: Not everyone agrees with you.

HOWARD: I shouldn't argue the point.

VERN: Well, I intend to profit by whatever opportunities present themselves.

HOWARD: You wouldn't get much.

VERN: No, I shall do well. I shall be a better man for my efforts. We are always better men for our efforts.

HOWARD: You will be worse for yours.

VERN: I don't intend to be.

HOWARD: Then you come here to give me advice and I'm asking why, when really I am hoping that you'd have got lost and were held up along the way, that you'd have had an accident and were run over and were disposed of. I've made requests and have asked to be left alone and I'm not asking for advice. I shall never be seeking out advice and you can understand why I wouldn't want to be confused needlessly.

VERN: Yes, but it never hurts to hear other opinions, for curiosity's sake, if for nothing else.

KEIR: He's upset.

HOWARD: A comparison between you and me.

KEIR: I shouldn't have invited you in.

HOWARD: ARE YOU LISTENING? LISTEN TO ME. NO ONE LISTENS TO ME.

KEIR: You are talking too loudly.

HOWARD: OUT. GET OUT. YOU'RE USELESS VERN. OUT. GO AWAY. STOP HANGING AROUND OUR HOUSE. I am not fading away so people can watch me wither. I am not here for other's amusment. I AM NOT SPEAKING FOR YOUR PLEASURE. NOR FOR MY OWN.

VERN: Then I'll come back and see how you are doing a little later. All right?

HOWARD: YOU ANT. YOU WORM. YOU'RE AN ANT IN A WORM HOLE VERN. YOU WORM. VERN YOU'RE A WORM. A SPINELESS WORM. A SQUIRMING SPINELESS MAGGOT GRUBBING WORM.

(Vern exits. Pause.)

Why is it that some people's problems are so insignificant, and others are so terrible it makes you weep to think of them?

KEIR: He may one day never come back and you will be sorry.

HOWARD: I am ready to go myself off to Holland. I'll get there if I have to swim. There are ways of going mad, I can reason myself into it. I can find the most logical reason ever thought of that makes no sense and lose my mind trying to understand what I meant. I fell asleep. I could fall asleep when I was a child with my eyes open staring at the sun, blinded by it... As a last resort. Unexpectedly to drop dead. Quietly disappear into an endless black void and nothing. One insightful visionary has enjoyed himself? If an apologist is laughing out loud. There's no ultimate hope to consider, not altogether, to hope for even optimistically. Except, if there is a peculiar reason to look on the bright side. Not a good reason to do so, philosophically, not yesterday and not the day before. Look at today. A sad old feeble-minded senior, elderly and senile, half-dead, still alive, yet soon to step out for good. On his last legs, barely standing, dead on his feet. A dead tired insomniac would have known that he was never going to rest in peace, not immortally, nor eternally. A catastrophe: an apocalypse. Nearby around the corner. Beyond the horizon: the future. Our inevitable destiny. Grim fate. No. We won't make it to the end. Because what is someone doing to get through the day and pass away into the night? Why does anyone half alive care about the past or the future when today and tomorrow and the day after. Sooner than expected: likely dead and gone forever. Or a young and inexperienced corpse has to tolerate it and live and a little humility and uncertainty, unimaginably humble and unassuming. Employed and hard at work, but no guarantees and no security, not gainfully employed and no financial monetary reward. Exploited. Persecuted by cynics. Sadistically dissected when alive. Over my dead body. But with assassins out hunting, homicidal executioners, cold-blooded murderers and bloodthirsty cannibals. Hunting us down inhumanely to tear us limb from limb in cold-blood and feast on our flesh and bones. That would probably humble a nihilist, who'd have to give up and accept ultimate fate. It's predetermined? Now I'm going to be humble — reliable and conscientious. God, humble me, good old God. God, humble me. No, I'm not open to being humble or humiliated for amusement. Though needless to say, there's no immediately available option other than to talk about myself to address the problem, the problem has to do with facts, science, mind... mind over matter. What matters. What makes a difference? Is there anything?

(She takes a note from a balloon.)

KEIR: All right, shall I put on some music? Would you

like to listen to some music? I'll put on some music.

HOWARD: Why?

KEIR: You've finished talking.

HOWARD: What music?

KEIR: It will soothe the beast inside of you.

HOWARD: Go ahead. Put on some music. Something horrible. Force me to listen to something that would make me wish I was deaf.

(Keir puts on a selection of dissonant music. Maybe Mists *by Iannis Xanakis.)*

Jesus, listen to that, and the cynic who wrote that. I wonder how he lives with himself. He's deaf and writes music for those who wish they were deaf.

KEIR: What does it remind you of, Howard?

HOWARD: Turn it off. Turn it off! Turn that off!

(She turns the music off. Pause.)

KEIR: I'd have thought you'd liked to have heard more.

HOWARD: No, maybe later. Why do I get upset for nothing? For nothing. To get excited about something I get upset.

KEIR: So don't get upset.

(She turns on music: Surrexit pastor bonus by Jean Lhéritier. They listen to it.)

But let me remind you of something.

HOWARD: Is it our song?

KEIR: It is.

HOWARD: Was it?

KEIR: We didn't have a song, Howard.

HOWARD: I had forgotten.

KEIR: Then I'll remind you. It was one day. We were walking along in a cemetery. The weather was fine. Birds were chirping. It was sunny. It had rained in the morning and desert flowers had come up. Children were playing hide-and-seek amongst the tombstones, and someone was being buried. A widow who was about my age. You could hear her weeping.

HOWARD: In the wind.

KEIR: I was thinking of having a child. I was thinking of having a child. You had gone off to play hide-and-seek with the children. And I remember thinking you would never be found again. You'd be lost. Those children would look for you, but they would never find you. *(pause)* It was a beautiful day, in a cemetery, and we were enjoying ourselves.

HOWARD: I was hiding in a freshly dug grave.

KEIR: The past always comes back. It comes back. I am coming back to get you. If I have to I will remind you of everything. I will remind you. Whatever your sins, I will remind you of them. Remember me. I'm God. It's me. Her voice. I am God. And you loved me.

(They listen until the song ends.)

HOWARD *(yawns)*: But something is wrong... I think... I'm... I am falling asleep.

KEIR: What?

HOWARD *(yawns)*: I can't keep awake. I am going to have to lie down.

KEIR: Lie down then.

HOWARD: I am falling asleep.

KEIR: Lie down.

HOWARD: But I shouldn't. I'd like to stay awake.

KEIR: You're falling asleep.

HOWARD: Don't let me fall asleep. I have to stay awake. This is no time to fall asleep.

KEIR: Shh.

HOWARD: Aaaah... *(He gets off his feet, lies down, spreads out on the floor.)* I can't stay awake. I'm tired. What were you saying? *(pause)* What?

KEIR: Nothing. Shh.

HOWARD: Ah.

KEIR: You're going to wake yourself up, shh.

(Howard mumbles incoherently.)

Are you asleep? Sleep.

HOWARD: Help.

KEIR: Sleep.

(Howard moans. Pause. A sound track of light snoring comes up and plays until indicated to stop. Knocking at the door.)

LOUISE *(offstage)*: Hello. The door is open.

(Enter Louise.)

KEIR *(whispering)*: Hello. He is sleeping. He fell asleep.

LOUISE: He's sleeping?

KEIR: Just fell asleep.

(He moans in his sleep.)

Finally.

LOUISE: Well.

KEIR: He just lay down and fell asleep.

(pause)

LOUISE: So my father has just passed away. *(pause)* He yawned and died. *(pause)* It was only a matter of when. *(pause)* I wanted to tell someone.

KEIR: Well, I am sorry.

LOUISE: It was just a matter of time. Then I have taken care of everything. Please don't send me a letter of condolence, though I would like to give you a letter of thanks, which is pre-emptive of me.

(She gives a letter to Keir.)

Go ahead and read it.

(She reads it.)

KEIR: You're relieved.

LOUISE: I am.

KEIR: I am sorry. If there is anything I can do.

LOUISE: Well, he's dead. There is nothing anyone can do.

KEIR: You are all right?

LOUISE: I'm fine.

KEIR *(humouring her)*: But I could send you a letter of condolence?

LOUISE: No, there is no need to. *(pause)* I am relaxed that it's over, and he's relaxed, too. *(Pointing to Howard.)* How everything is changing so quickly, it seems.

KEIR: Yes.

LOUISE: It's an odd place to sleep. Is he comfortable?

KEIR: As long as he sleeps.

LOUISE: He looks uncomfortable.

KEIR: I wouldn't want to move him. He might wake up.

LOUISE: But to leave him there like that.

KEIR: He'll be fine.

LOUISE: Does he need a blanket?

KEIR: No, he would get too hot.

LOUISE: But on the floor he might get a little cold.

KEIR: No, he never sleeps with a blanket. *(pause)* I suspect he will sleep for days.

LOUISE: Then you'll have to move him probably.

KEIR: I'll let him sleep as long as he wants.

LOUISE: He's an energetic man not to have slept for so long.

KEIR: He is that and other things, and when we met I thought at first that he was the uncomplicated kind of man.

LOUISE: Those are the ones that are the hardest to understand.

KEIR: He used to get excited about important things, now it's the little things that bother him.

LOUISE: That's a common problem.

KEIR: It is.

LOUISE: There's nothing we can do for them.

KEIR: You appreciate it's not easy.

LOUISE: I know, men are funny animals.

(Howard grunts.)

KEIR: He dreams like a dog, and he's wagging his tail.

(Howard comfortably moans.)

He is thinking of what he always wanted, and wouldn't ever have admitted what that might have been.

LOUISE: They never do.

KEIR: Never?

LOUISE: When I was younger. I used to tell men I wasn't the woman of their dreams and I wasn't. "No, no, it's not me. She's younger; the one you're looking for." But I was still young then, but then our powers of seduction abandon us. It is sad to see them go.

KEIR: It is sad.

LOUISE: I wasted them.

KEIR: Ah.

LOUISE: I used to believe that I could have any of them

that pleased me. But they were somehow less than what was to be hoped for.

KEIR: Yes.

LOUISE: There was always something. They didn't know how to eat or talked too much, said nothing.

KEIR: Men are beasts.

LOUISE: Our poor mothers.

KEIR: I worry about the children.

LOUISE: So do I.

KEIR: Our poor children.

LOUISE: I know.

KEIR: But what can we do?

LOUISE: I don't know.

KEIR: But watch the harm that's done.

THERESA *(offstage and through the window)*: Hello. It's me.

(Theresa comes in.)

KEIR *(whispering)*: Shh, he's fallen asleep. Just fell asleep.

THERESA: Asleep? He should be put to sleep.

KEIR *(whispering)*: Shh.

THERESA: Are you sure? He's asleep, well —

KEIR: Shh.

THERESA: Look at that, and you should get rid of him. Have him removed and thrown out.

(Knocking at the door.)

VERN *(offstage)*: Hello. I can come in, shall I close the door?

(Vern looks in through the window.)

KEIR: Yes.

VERN: Hello, I was afraid I annoyed Howard more than I wanted. I should like to apologize. *(Enter Vern: noticing Howard.)* What is it?

KEIR: He's sleeping.

THERESA: If I could I'd haul him off for you.

VERN: Asleep?

THERESA: Leave him in a ditch somewhere.

VERN: He's really asleep?

THERESA: How could you have stayed with him for so long?

VERN: Yes, he is a hard man to do business with.

THERESA: Why? Is what I don't understand.

LOUISE: There are much worse. I can testify to that.

THERESA: And what to do with these men who go after power and will stop at nothing to get it?

VERN: There is nothing wrong with power, it's the use of it that is the problem.

THERESA: Give it to the wrong people and they destroy everything.

VERN: Some do, but not everyone.

THERESA: He is the kind that would destroy everything.

KEIR: Please.

THERESA: You should save yourself, and how many times have I said that?

(Knocking at the door. The noise of the knocking is lower and resonant.)

KEIR: Excuse me.

(Keir moves to exit.)

THERESA: Look at him. You'd think he was at peace with himself.

KEIR *(to the person knocking)*: Just a minute.

(Loud knocking. Howard moans. Keir exits.)

THERESA: He is probably having a nightmare and it doesn't even wake him up.

KEIR *(offstage)*: Hello, no, no. Sorry. *(To those onstage.)* There is a man who's asking for some money, who needs help. He is begging for it.

VERN: What's that?

KEIR *(to those onstage)*: I've nothing, but if any of you have something I could offer him, maybe then he will go away.

LOUISE: No, I don't have anything.

VERN: No, I don't think so.

KEIR *(offstage)*: No I am very sorry.

VERN: I don't have any to spare at the moment.

KEIR *(offstage)*: Look we have nothing. You are becoming a problem. I said we have nothing. No.

(There is a scuffle at the door.)

KEIR: He won't take no for an answer.

VERN: Beggars are becoming a problem.

KEIR *(offstage)*: Nothing. No change. Nothing.

VERN: Howard was telling me about you.

THERESA: I don't know you.

VERN: Friend of the family.

THERESA: So am I, and I try to help. But you can imagine what good that does. I don't know what I try to do.

(Howard moans in his sleep. Keir re-enters.)

I'd kill him for you if I could.

VERN: I could find someone who would.

KEIR: Really?

(Howard moans.)

THERESA: He should be put out of his misery. That would be the greatest kindness you could do for him.

VERN: I could bury him for you.

LOUISE: I'll make the arrangements.

THERESA: The worst is that you know he wouldn't appreciate us joking at his expense. All he does is laugh at others.

(Loud knocking.)

KEIR: That man. I can't get rid of him. Vern, could you help?

VERN: I'll do it.

(Vern picks up a large stone from the pile. Exits.)

VERN: God-damn these people.

THERESA: He's the one to get rid of.

VERN *(offstage)*: Go on.

(A commotion is heard offstage.)

THERESA: At least I tried. What is going on out there? There is always fighting when I come here. Always a disagreement. I don't know why I waste my time coming here. I waste my time. I knew that before I came, didn't I?

(Theresa exits. Noise of fighting outside.)

LOUISE: They are fighting.

KEIR: What a world.

THERESA *(offstage)*: Get out of my way. Go on! Out of my way!

LOUISE: She'll take care of him.

THERESA *(offstage)*: You scum. Go back to the slum where you belong.

KEIR: She will.

(They listen to the outside noise.)

LOUISE: God Almighty.

KEIR: I hope they don't wake him up.

(Sound of pots breaking.)

Your pots?

LOUISE: That will save me from breaking them myself.

(Noise gets louder.)

LOUISE: If that doesn't wake him up nothing will.

KEIR: He's not always a sound sleeper.

(Explosion. Silence. Sound of snoring continues.)

LOUISE: What happened?

KEIR: Oh.

LOUISE: What was that noise?

KEIR: The end of it.

LOUISE: Sounded like it.

KEIR: It's over anyway, for now.

LOUISE: But what could have happened?

KEIR: I don't know.

LOUISE: So I suppose, I would really like to be honest with you.

KEIR: No need to be, please.

LOUISE: I suppose not.

KEIR: No.

(pause)

LOUISE: Well, I ought to go and see to the arrangements.

KEIR: If there is anything.

LOUISE: Thank you.

KEIR: May I ask you to tell Vern that I would like Howard to be in peace. Tell him we will see him later maybe.

LOUISE: Yes.

KEIR: Bye.

(Louise exits.)

Shh. Everything is fine. Don't worry. *(Keir gets down on her knees. Puts Howard's head in her lap.)* Sleep, and if you are in there and can hear me. I know you can. You are in there somewhere listening. Sleep now. Sleep. It's God speaking to you. Sleep now. Sleep. And when you wake up, but sleep.

(A number of bicycle bells ring offstage.)

ACT III

(Bicycle bells ring offstage. Snoring stops. He wakes up.)

HOWARD: Ah.

KEIR: Shh.

HOWARD: I am at home.

KEIR: Where else would you be?

HOWARD: I haven't lost my mind. Have I?

KEIR: Not that I can see.

HOWARD: I don't remember.

KEIR: You slept. I was afraid I was going to have to wake you. How do you feel?

HOWARD: Rested. I was dreaming, dreaming of, I was dreaming that I was in the clouds and I was talking with a man, a man who was—he was a saint and we entered into a discussion on theology, until it started to lead nowhere, and then.

KEIR: Yes?

HOWARD: I want to tell you this?

KEIR: I'm listening.

HOWARD: There was a dog, someone said it was a Chinese dog, it was a black dog, it was barking at the saint who I was talking to, he called his name, the dog's name, not the saint's, the saint called the dog's name—Hegel, the dog's name that is, not the saint's. It was an odd coincidence. Hegel means black dog in Chinese. So there was a pig. It flew up to me. It had wings, and the dog ran off. The pig was begging to be fed as if it were a dog. I didn't give the animal anything to eat and it died of starvation, while I sat on a cloud stuffing my face with truffles. Pigs love truffles. *(pause)* That's my dream. My first dream since I can remember. What does it mean? Nothing. I have the first dream that I have had in a long time and it means nothing and now I am afraid to forget it. I am going to forget it.

KEIR: If you like I can remember it for you.

HOWARD: But I would be better off to remember it myself.

KEIR: Perhaps you would be.

HOWARD: Is someone here?

KEIR: We are alone.

HOWARD: It's nice to be alone.

KEIR: We're alone.

HOWARD: Then our friends, so how are they?

KEIR: As you were sleeping they asked about you.

HOWARD: I imagine they would have. Our friends are funny people.

KEIR: They are, yes. They've had their disappointments, like us.

HOWARD: That is true.

KEIR: Louise's father died.

HOWARD: He died?

KEIR: In his sleep.

HOWARD: No one dies in their sleep. They always wake up the moment before. We wake up to die.

KEIR: I don't think he woke up. She said he yawned and died.

HOWARD: If he yawned he was waking up.

KEIR: Either way he's dead.

(pause)

HOWARD: But what are we doing on the floor?

KEIR: Would you like to get up? Go outside. It'd be good for you.

HOWARD: No, I'll stay here.

KEIR: I could blindfold you and then we'll go out. When you're ready.

HOWARD: Then someone's coming.

(Knocking at door.)

VERN *(offstage)*: Hello.

(Enter Vern.)

HOWARD: Vern?

VERN: Then you're awake.

HOWARD: Yes.

VERN: Good to have a sleep after all that time.

HOWARD: It did me some good.

VERN: Well, then the way things are going it doesn't look like anyone will ever sleep too much again. So now there's a break from the past that is occurring as far as we can see, and the time has never been as right to meet a new future challenge and the future won't be like the old one.

HOWARD: I hope not.

VERN: Not even remotely.

HOWARD: I hope so.

VERN: The times are not reasonable. Then already it is nearly impossible to keep track of what's happening, and you know under these circumstances that's when there are opportunities that come up and we chase after them and hunt them down.

HOWARD: I just woke up. What did you say? I am not following you.

VERN: I'd do you a good turn, Howard.

HOWARD: A good turn?

VERN: On my honour.

HOWARD: A noble sentiment.

VERN: If sincere.

HOWARD: What are you talking about?

KEIR: He's teasing you, Howard.

HOWARD: Don't tease me, Vern.

VERN: No, no.

HOWARD: There is no need for it.

VERN: No time for it and what is happening is —

HOWARD: Please.

VERN: Is that we're witnessing events that are promising change for those who are in need of it, individually as well as collectively, of course, for you and everyone.

HOWARD: Good.

VERN: Then I am proposing to you assistance, then free travel to a place of safe haven.

HOWARD: I'm not following you.

VERN: You'll follow the others, a group will come by and you'll go with them.

HOWARD: Follow who? *(To Keir.)* What is he saying? What's this about? What is this?

VERN: Populations are leaving their lives behind. It's a migration that has begun.

HOWARD: I don't understand, Vern.

VERN: We're leaving our homes, our families, our friends to maybe meet at another time if we have to and if we're lucky.

HOWARD: Oh, then when would that be?

VERN: Sooner or later, I would suspect is the idea.

HOWARD: So I can understand that not having a clear idea is interesting, but why not have some idea, if I can ask what it is.

VERN: You would prefer a clear explanation?

HOWARD: No.

VERN: Well, it's not a picture to admire objectively nor subjectively. There have been fires, disappearances that remain unexplained. Random acts of violence. Mysterious deaths. Then no place will be safe before long.

HOWARD: Then why go anywhere else if no place is safe?

VERN: But stay, then maybe you will be taken to already be dead or stay and wait to be killed. I could arrange so that you would be.

HOWARD: I might well be. I had terrible dreams.

KEIR: We could go.

HOWARD *(to Keir)*: Go? Where?

VERN: We're leaving. It's happening, everything that many have hoped for and expected and waited for. But you can stay. Be left behind. Live in the past and soon you will be a part of what is left behind in the past.

HOWARD: But what is wrong with being a part of the past? What's wrong with it?

VERN: I couldn't say.

HOWARD: What's wrong with it?

VERN: I can't answer that. Good day.

(Keir accompanies Vern to the door. She exits with him.)

HOWARD *(calling after Vern)*: There is nothing wrong with it! There are a lot of people who would be better off in the past!

(Keir re-enters.)

But what am I arguing about?

KEIR: We will go out.

HOWARD: Don't let me argue.

KEIR: We can go. I'll blindfold you. Close your eyes. You're still half asleep, Howard. You're almost asleep? So take my arm now.

(He takes her arm. She leads him a few steps. Music comes on. It is dissonant.)

HOWARD: The music, that will make me want to leave. Yes.

(They circle around in one spot. She stands behind him, puts her hands over his eyes.)

KEIR: Close your eyes. I'm blindfolding you.

HOWARD: There's light coming through. You have to close the window.

KEIR: Close your eyes!

HOWARD: I see light.

KEIR: Then at least you're not as blind as you might seem to be most of the time.

(They turn around.)

Does any of this look at all familiar to you?

HOWARD: I can't tell one way or another, Keir.

KEIR: I believe we're coming to a graveyard.

HOWARD: We are? Really?

KEIR: We could avoid it maybe.

HOWARD: No.

KEIR: You wouldn't believe it. There's a church next to it. It looks like it's on fire. *(She removes her hands.)*

We'll go inside. We'll say a few prayers. You can pray. Ask for something.

HOWARD: If you'd like.

KEIR: It never hurts to ask.

HOWARD: Or maybe it does hurt to ask, if the answer is incorrect.

(A cloud of balloons falls on them and perhaps into the audience. Volume of the music fades.)

KEIR: There are balloons falling.

(She looks at the notes attached to the balloons. He stands with his eyes closed. Voices of children playing are heard.)

HOWARD: I've lost my mind? I'll pray to get it back.

KEIR: They're blank.

HOWARD: All right, I'm praying now. I never thought I would. Then I might admit that I have been difficult at times and I have no excuses, but I can't help but think of a few. So it seems to me that I haven't made any difference.

KEIR: No one has. I haven't either.

HOWARD: But you have.

KEIR: I haven't.

HOWARD: Then I want to apologize for anything and everything, if I can. Then I have slept. I have had a dream. I seem to have gone out with you. I've apologized. Who knows what I'll do next?

KEIR: You do.

HOWARD: I should. I don't. *(He holds her in his arms.)* So how's this?

(He kisses her. The kiss is not sentimentally successful.)

I've tried to kiss you. Then it would be nice, if we were in a church to enjoy ourselves.

KEIR: No, Howard.

HOWARD: I'd like to apologize again, and you know it's true that it's easier to apologize than to get permission.

KEIR: We must go somewhere else now.

HOWARD: I'd like to stay here. Watch the place burn down. *(pause)* I had forgotten what a church looked like. It's the same as I remember. They haven't changed. Why is it churches never change?

(They resume turning around. Sound of one bicycle bell is heard, joined by thousands of bicycle bells ringing, the noise passes, disappearing into the distance. The ringing returns, circles around them. Thousands of bicycle horns honk. From another direction, one bicycle bell is heard, then a thousand bells are heard, quickly passing. A bicycle horn honks.)

Then if we were on a bike for two, you would steer and I would pedal. Do you think that anyone has an idea of what has happened?

KEIR: Not completely.

HOWARD: It's reassuring to know that.

KEIR: Yes.

HOWARD: But to have some idea would also be reassuring.

(Vern rides in. White balloons are attached to his bicycle. He circles around them. Exits. Enter Theresa. She remains apart from the action. She stares out.)

Then how long has it been since the last act of creation? Why am I asking that all of the sudden? What the hell am I talking about?

KEIR: I don't think it matters.

HOWARD: It doesn't matter. That is it, of course. But hasn't everything always been that way? Hasn't it?

KEIR: Sh.

HOWARD: I shouldn't be talking so much.

KEIR: No, you shouldn't.

HOWARD: You could say more. I'd say less from time to time.

KEIR: No, I couldn't, because someone has to be quiet.

HOWARD: I suppose so. I should be.

KEIR: Then I have nothing to say at the moment.

HOWARD: Nothing.

THERESA *(addressing no one)*: Neither do I.

(Theresa exits. Vern bicycles by. Howard and Keir walk around through the balloons on the floor.)

HOWARD: But here we are. What do we do? Now what?

KEIR: I don't know.

HOWARD: That could be anything.

KEIR: Think of something useful if you can.

HOWARD: That could be anything, too.

KEIR: No, it is either useful or it's not.

HOWARD: We might as well relax and let anything happen and not get excited. Then when rested, but we're never rested, as much as we might be.

KEIR: Quiet.

HOWARD *(whispering)*: All right, I'll be quiet. We were trying to say something else. If I understand. *(Stops whispering.)* What it is? I don't know. Maybe I am not sure. I mean, do we remember? When we look back to the day. I am talking about.

KEIR: Be quiet!

HOWARD: It's not certain if we want to understand much, that much we suspect is probably true.

KEIR: For God's sake!

HOWARD: I've always said more than I should have.

KEIR: Yes.

HOWARD: Yet nothing really.

KEIR: That's right.

(Keir opens the window. Enter Louise. She is tattered in appearance, her clothes are torn, she moves lifelessly. She has suffered an indignity.)

Hello.

LOUISE: I hope I am not intruding. Could I ask if you have anything to eat? I am hungry. I am very hungry. I'm dying of hunger.

HOWARD: But you look well.

LOUISE: I am very hungry. Can you believe it? A funeral director, an undertaker tried to assault me. He said I was a tease.

HOWARD: So we'll have to get something to eat and we'll have a feast and get drunk and our inhibitions will be released. Yes, why not?

(A gong is struck. Enter Vern dressed opulently in a suit. He positions himself to gain attention. He declaims.)

VERN: Excuse me for interrupting. Then I am glad to see that you are happy to see me because I didn't know if you'd be pleased to have a visit so soon since we spoke last, and I never know who will or won't be happy to see me and I can understand why. And now, well now, I have a hard time believing in my own good fortune, which comes easier for some than for others. Then I've done very well. I have made a handy sum of money, which I do intend to put to work and you see, the time has come for us all to see what we can do. And you know, I remember all the discussions we had and I'd hate to think they were not useful. So I shall have a chance to put some of my theories into practice and I intend to spend what I have to accomplish what I can, until I've nothing left. You can maybe laugh at me, but I will succeed where others have been less successful. I will do what hasn't been done in the past. Maybe I'm wrong, but I'll find out. But in any case, I intend to put up a good fight. It's an adventure. There's always one out there somewhere. So I've come to ask Keir to come along with me, as we're looking for those who can organize and move people, influence them, make decisions, execute them. Administrate things properly. She has been conscribed.

KEIR: Yes, I can be of help.

VERN: Then we are all going to continue challenging old assumptions since we don't have to believe in going on in the same way as before and that case has been made by a number of interesting realizations that have and will continue to come to light, as time goes by. *(To Keir.)* If you want, I can step out and wait. I'll wait outside while you say farewell and goodbye once and for all.

(Vern exits.)

HOWARD: I feel, I feel somehow detached.

KEIR: It's not a question of what anyone feels.

(Keir exits. Pause.)

HOWARD: It looks like my wife has left.

LOUISE: Could I stay?

HOWARD: Yes. *(pause)* My wife has just left me under very strange circumstances. I can only hope it's for the best.

(Special on rock comes up. Lights dim.)

That rock. It reminds me of a rock someone threw at me once.

LOUISE: It fell from the sky.

HOWARD: I'm surprised it didn't land on my head.

LOUISE: The sun has set.

HOWARD: They should have taken those balloons with them. *(He gently kicks the balloons about.)* I had a passion for balloons when I was a child. I would blow them up until they burst in my face. Shall we remain in the dark?

LOUISE: I can't stand any more.

HOWARD: You're lying on the table?

LOUISE: I am lying.

HOWARD: Are you?

LOUISE: Come here, Howard. Come over here. I've a flower for you. I am starving. If I bite you it's because I am hungry.

HOWARD: You are trying to bite me?

LOUISE: I am hungry. I'm starving.

HOWARD: We'll find some food afterwards, but first.

LOUISE: I am faint.

HOWARD: You'll be hungrier later.

(A wisp of light comes in through the window.)

I am hungry myself. We'll have a feast.

LOUISE: A feast.

HOWARD: Prepared for us specially. Then we'll eat until we are sick.

LOUISE: Yes.

HOWARD: I know a cook. A master chef, I'll have him in to cook for us. He'll cater for us while we are in bed.

(Knocking at the door. Low pitch sounding knock.)

LOUISE: When?

HOWARD: Soon. We can get in bed and wait for him to come. Then a messenger will arrive from the kitchen and tell us there is more than enough to eat and we can eat whatever we want and we'll stuff ourselves with all that we could possibly eat, with lamb and beef, wild boar and roasted venison, and rabbit pie *(knocking)* and orange sunset yams reminding you that this is the last meal of the day, and fresh baked Belgian bread nutted with acorns taken from the winter stock of young squirrels, dipped in musk-scented liquors and sodden with Portuguese sherry and quickly washed down with Spanish brandy accompanied by a dish of bog-berries scented with mushrooms taken from the dunghills of heifers, served up with firm strong frog legs from the winners of every frog jumping contest on the continent. *(knocking)* And baked potatoes cooked in a pit of hot marble rocks from Greek ruins. Yellow custards like the sun at dawn. I used to write menus. When I was young I was a great writer of menus!

LOUISE: Stop.

HOWARD: But there is a moral problem.

LOUISE: If I don't eat...

HOWARD: Then I should start collecting rocks again, look for my tombstone. Are you all right? No, you're not.

LOUISE: Call your chef.

HOWARD: He's probably in his kitchen, cooking with food that would have been given to orphans. I find food tastes better when you know someone else can't have it. So my friend, the cook, he'll be in the kitchen, cooking for the time-being, not too long. He will die of food poisoning.

(Knocking at the door, higher in pitch. Howard picks up the rock from the table and throws it onto the rock pile.)

I must get rid of that pile. I must get rid of them. I will throw them one by one over the horizon and watch them disappear. I'll get rid of them. I will. But first I'll have something to eat, clean the place up, and then get some sleep. But am I worried about becoming convinced by past experience? Is that something to worry about? For example.

(Enter Theresa.)

THERESA: It's not too late?

HOWARD: I was wondering. What's relevant.

(Knocking.)

THERESA: I came in to see if you were going to answer your door?

HOWARD: I should.

THERESA: There was a time when you and I and our family and friends wanted to do everyone a favour.

(Knocking less urgent.)

All right, I'll answer it then.

HOWARD: No, there's no point.

THERESA: Maybe there isn't. But I will answer it anyway, say there is no one home?

(Theresa exits.)

LOUISE: Is someone there?

HOWARD: No. We're not here. Everyone should have run for cover.

(Knocking. He picks up a white balloon. Lights and knocking fade out. Downstage perhaps, enter Vern and Keir.)

VERN: Then you've said goodbye to a soon-to-be dead man probably.

KEIR: I have.

VERN: So maybe when a person doesn't have long for this world it's easy to say goodbye.

KEIR: It wasn't too difficult.

VERN: I don't think I had much advice to really offer. Did I?

KEIR: I gathered that.

VERN: Yes, I guess that new prospects are never well received.

KEIR: But Vern, you don't actually believe in a future. I suspect you don't.

VERN: I do. I think so.

KEIR: Oh?

VERN: I think you might know why. We have to. What other choice do we have? Yet even if we don't, what's important, is the starting point, so we have the idea to get on with it and run and the idea being that there's a better story. We tell it as it is, it'll come, the story to tell. So then the future, we want to live to see the day and then how we will strive for a better life and hope for it at the least. How we will conquer the world one day: good over evil. How we will become good and better people, the kind of people we hope to be, sane, kind and considerate, helpful and caring and loving, interested in justice for all. I don't know. Of course, after all the garbage has been flushed out of the system. That has to happen first.

KEIR: You believe that?

VERN: I do. I do.

KEIR: I'm not convinced. I have reasons not to be.

VERN: Then the outcome will be that no one will be the same as we always were. That's for sure.

KEIR: How's that?

VERN: It's possible and why not?

KEIR: That will never happen.

VERN: That's what has to change. So one day none of us will be what we were, not the same as always.

KEIR: How's that possible?

VERN: We'll be enlightened and what we're doing will make sense, as if we knew what we were doing and I am pretty sure about that now. I know I am.

KEIR: No. I am not convinced.

VERN: You will be, Keir. You will be. You will be.

KEIR: I doubt it.

VERN: You'll have no choice not to be.

KEIR: I'd rather have a choice.

VERN: Maybe no choice is better if there isn't a better one.

KEIR: I'd rather have a choice.

VERN: Of course, I know what you mean. But what is it?

KEIR: Yes, that's the problem. Because really I'm tired of listening to too many men. You talk and talk, but promise what? What do you promise? All men and women ever do is promise to talk more. That's all you ever do. But what do any of you have to say for yourselves, any of you? Nothing worth listening to any more. The game is up, but it always has been. It's over. Then now there's not much left to save.

(Blackout.)

Curtain

www.ingramcontent.com/pod-product-compliance
Ingram Content Group UK Ltd.
Pitfield, Milton Keynes, MK11 3LW, UK
UKHW020417250726
13967UKWH00007B/2698